Sing-Along
NURSERY
RHYMES

hinkler

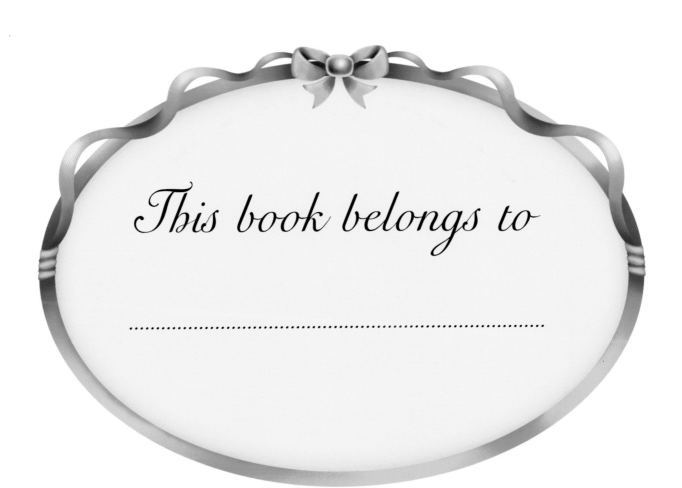

This book belongs to

....

Sing-Along
Nursery
Rhymes

Published by Hinkler Books Pty Ltd
45–55 Fairchild Street
Heatherton Victoria 3202 Australia
www.hinkler.com.au

hinkler

Hinkler Books Pty Ltd 2012

Illustrations, Design and Layout © Hinkler Books Pty Ltd 2012
Sound Recording © Love to Sing Ltd, Linda Adamson 2012
Arrangements © Love to Sing Ltd, Linda Adamson 2012

www.childrenlovetosing.com

Cover Design: Hinkler Design Studio
Cover Illustration: Mirela Tufan
Illustrators: Andrew Hopgood, Melissa Webb, Gerad Taylor,
Geoff Cook, Bill Wood, Anton Petrov and Marten Coombe
Prepress: Graphic Print Group

ISBN: 978 1 7430 8852 4

Printed and bound in China

Contents

Contents

I'm a Little Teapot

I'm a little teapot, short and stout,
Here is my handle, here is my spout.
When I get all steamed up, hear me shout,
'Tip me up and pour me out.'

JACK AND JILL

Jack and Jill went up the hill
To fetch a pail of water;
Jack fell down and broke his crown,
And Jill came tumbling after.

Up Jack got and home did trot
As fast as he could caper;
He went to bed to mend his head
With vinegar and brown paper.

OLD MCDONALD HAD A FARM

Old McDonald had a farm,
E-I-E-I-O!
And on that farm he had some cows,
E-I-E-I-O!
With a moo-moo here, and a moo-moo there,
Here a moo, there a moo,
Everywhere a moo-moo!
Old McDonald had a farm,
E-I-E-I-O!

Old McDonald had a farm,
E-I-E-I-O!
And on that farm he had some chickens,
E-I-E-I-O!
With a chick-chick here, and a chick-chick there,
Here a chick, there a chick,
Everywhere a chick-chick!
Old McDonald had a farm,
E-I-E-I-O!

Old McDonald had a farm,
E-I-E-I-O!
And on that farm he had some pigs,
E-I-E-I-O!
With an oink-oink here, and an oink-oink there,
Here an oink, there an oink,
Everywhere an oink-oink!
Old McDonald had a farm,
E-I-E-I-O!

Old McDonald had a farm,
E-I-E-I-O!
And on that farm he had some sheep,
E-I-E-I-O!
With a baa-baa here,
 and a baa-baa there,
Here a baa, there a baa,
Everywhere a baa-baa!
Old McDonald had a farm,
E-I-E-I-O!

Old McDonald had a farm,
E-I-E-I-O!
And on that farm he had some horses,
E-I-E-I-O!
With a neigh-neigh here,
 and a neigh-neigh there,
Here a neigh, there a neigh,
Everywhere a neigh-neigh!
Old McDonald had a farm,
E-I-E-I-O!

A SAILOR WENT TO SEA, SEA, SEA

A sailor went to sea, sea, sea,
To see what he could see, see, see;
But all that he could see, see, see,
Was the bottom of the deep blue sea, sea, sea!

Repeat

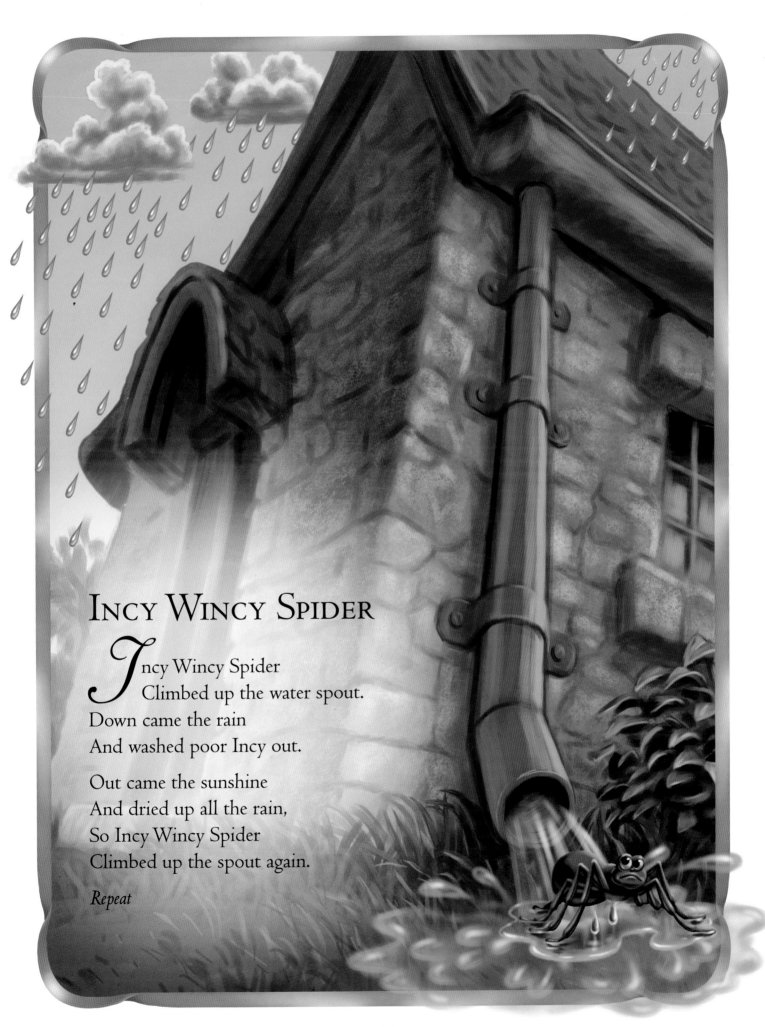

INCY WINCY SPIDER

Incy Wincy Spider
    Climbed up the water spout.
Down came the rain
And washed poor Incy out.

Out came the sunshine
And dried up all the rain,
So Incy Wincy Spider
Climbed up the spout again.

Repeat

HUMPTY DUMPTY

Humpty Dumpty sat on a wall,
Humpty Dumpty had a great fall;
All the king's horses and all the king's men
Couldn't put Humpty together again.

Repeat

Again, again,
Couldn't put Humpty
together again.

THREE BLIND MICE

Three blind mice, three blind mice!
   See how they run, see how they run!
They all ran after the farmer's wife,
Who cut off their tails with a carving knife;
Did you ever see such a thing in your life,
As three blind mice?

Repeat (as a round)

YANKEE DOODLE

*Y*ankee Doodle came to town,
Riding on a pony;
He stuck a feather in his cap
And called it macaroni.

Repeat three times

HICKORY, DICKORY, DOCK

Hickory, dickory, dock,
The mouse ran up the clock,
The clock struck one,
The mouse ran down,
Hickory, dickory, dock.

Hickory, dickory, dare,
The pig flew up in the air,
The man in the moon,
Sent him down quite soon,
Hickory, dickory, dare.

POP GOES THE WEASEL!

Up and down the City Road,
In and out the Eagle,
That's the way the money goes,
Pop goes the weasel!

Half a pound of tuppenny rice,
Half a pound of treacle,
Mix it up and make it nice,
Pop goes the weasel!

Every night when I go out
The monkey's on the table,
Take a stick and knock it off,
Pop goes the weasel!

MARY HAD A LITTLE LAMB

Mary had a little lamb,
Little lamb, little lamb;
Mary had a little lamb,
Its fleece was white as snow.

And everywhere that Mary went,
Mary went, Mary went;
And everywhere that Mary went,
The lamb was sure to go.

It followed her to school one day,
School one day, school one day;
It followed her to school one day,
That was against the rules.

It made the children laugh and play,
Laugh and play, laugh and play;
It made the children laugh and play,
To see a lamb at school.

HEY, DIDDLE, DIDDLE

Hey, diddle, diddle, the cat and the fiddle,
The cow jumped over the moon;
The little dog laughed to see such fun,
And the dish ran away with the spoon.

Repeat

BAA, BAA, BLACK SHEEP

Baa, baa, black sheep,
Have you any wool?
Yes, sir, yes, sir,
Three bags full;
One for the master,
One for the dame,
And one for the little boy
Who lives down the lane.

LITTLE MISS MUFFET

Little Miss Muffet
Sat on a tuffet,
Eating her curds and whey;
There came a big spider,
Who sat down beside her
And frightened
Miss Muffet away.

Little Miss Muffet
Sat on a tuffet,
Eating her curds and whey;
There came a big spider,
Who sat down beside her
And became her good friend that day.

RAIN, RAIN, GO AWAY

Rain, rain, go away,
Come again some other day.
Rain, rain, go away,
Come again some other day.

IT'S RAINING, IT'S POURING

*I*t's raining, it's pouring,
The old man is snoring;
He went to bed and bumped his head
And couldn't get up in the morning.

Repeat

See-saw

See-saw, Margery Daw,
   Jacky shall have a new master;
He shall have but a penny a day,
Because he can't work any faster.

Repeat

Ring-a-ring o' roses

Ring-a-ring o' roses
A pocket full of posies;
A-tishoo! A-tishoo!
We all fall down.

Ring-a-ring o' roses
A pocket full of posies;
A-tishoo! A-tishoo!
We all fall down.

LONDON BRIDGE

London Bridge is falling down,
Falling down, falling down.
London Bridge is falling down,
My fair lady.

Build it up with iron bars,
Iron bars, iron bars,
Build it up with iron bars,
My fair lady.

Iron bars will bend and break,
Bend and break, bend and break,
Iron bars will bend and break,
My fair lady.

Build it up with pins and needles,
Pins and needles, pins and needles,
Build it up with pins and needles,
My fair lady.

Pins and needles will rust and bend,
Rust and bend, rust and bend,
Pins and needles will rust and bend,
My fair lady.

Build it up with gravel and stone,
Gravel and stone, gravel and stone,
Build it up with gravel and stone,
My fair lady.

Gravel and stone will wash away,
Wash away, wash away,
Gravel and stone will wash away,
My fair lady.

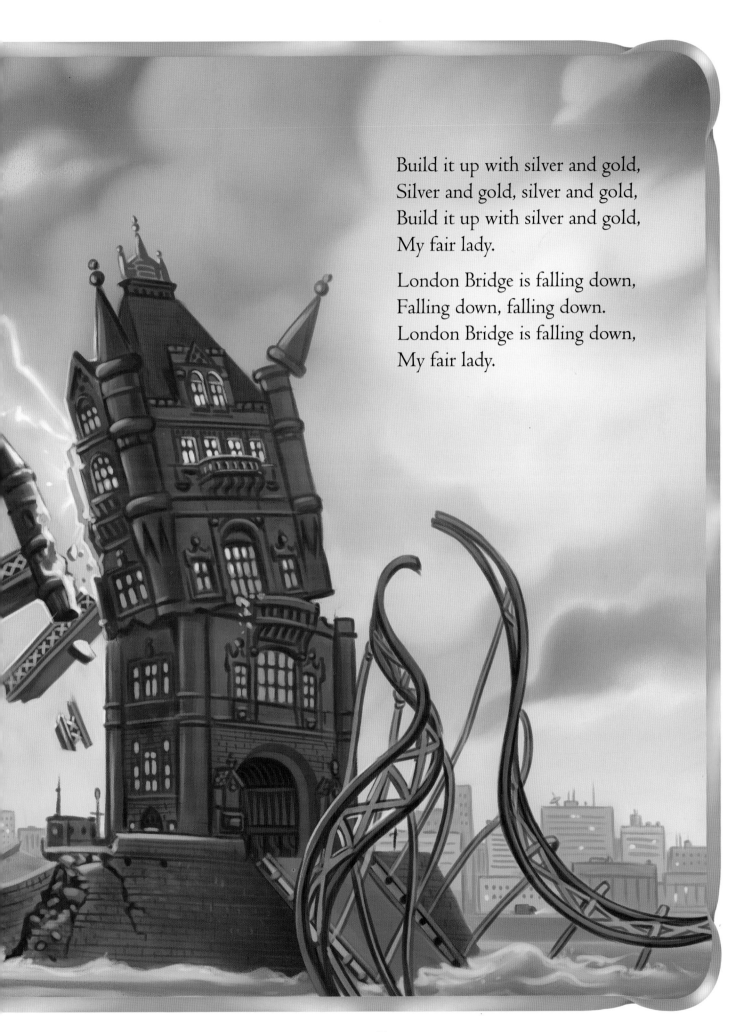

Build it up with silver and gold,
Silver and gold, silver and gold,
Build it up with silver and gold,
My fair lady.

London Bridge is falling down,
Falling down, falling down.
London Bridge is falling down,
My fair lady.

Mary, Mary, quite contrary

Mary, Mary, quite contrary,
How does your garden grow?
With silver bells and cockle shells,
And pretty maids all in a row.
And pretty maids all in a row.

Hot cross buns!

Hot cross buns!
Hot cross buns!
One a penny, two a penny,
Hot cross buns!

If you have no daughters,
Give them to your sons.
One a penny, two a penny,
Hot cross buns!

Repeat

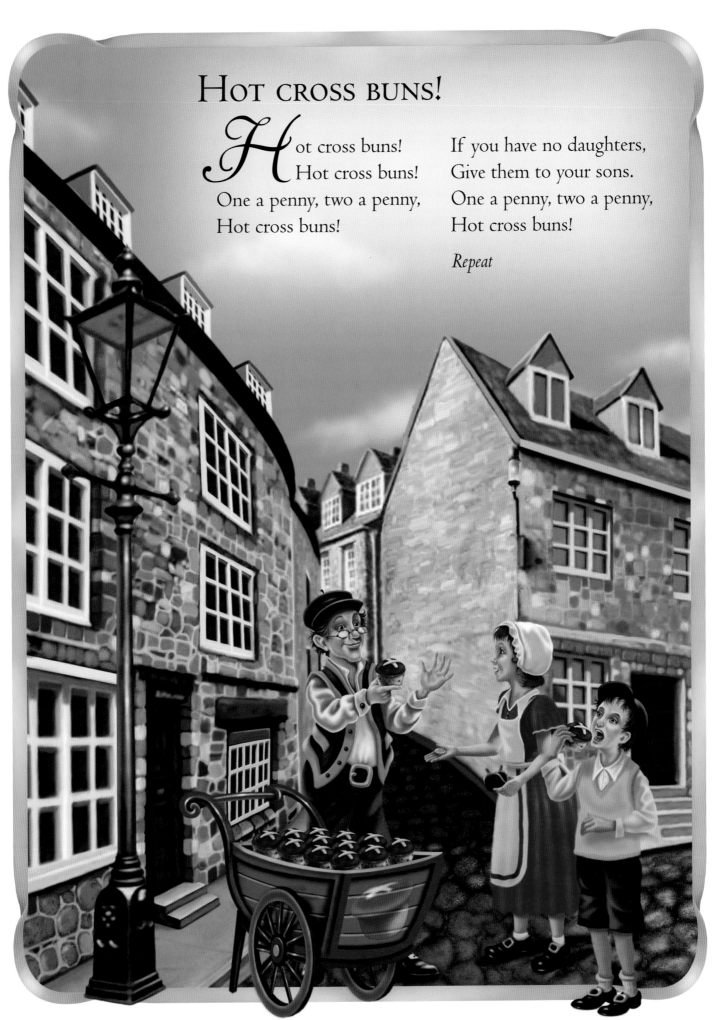

OLD KING COLE

Old King Cole
    Was a merry old soul,
And a merry old soul was he.
He called for his pipe,
And he called for his bowl,
And he called for his fiddlers three.
Every fiddler, he had a fiddle,
And a very fine fiddle had he;
Twee tweedle dee, tweedle dee,
    went the fiddlers.
Oh, there's none so rare,
As can compare
With King Cole and
    his fiddlers three.

OH WHERE, OH WHERE, HAS MY LITTLE DOG GONE?

Oh where, oh where,
Has my little dog gone?
Oh where, oh where can he be?

With his ears cut short
And his tail cut long,
Oh where, oh where is he?

Repeat

OLD MOTHER HUBBARD

Old Mother Hubbard
    Went to the cupboard
To fetch her poor dog a bone;
But when she got there,
The cupboard was bare,
And so the poor dog had none.

She went to the baker's
To buy him some bread;
But when she came back
The poor dog was dead.

She went to the undertaker's
To buy him a coffin;
But when she came back
The poor dog was laughing.

She went to the fishmonger's
To buy him some fish;
But when she came back
He was washing the dish.

She went to the tavern
For white wine and red;
But when she came back
The dog stood on his head.

She went to the hatter's
To buy him a hat;
But when she came back
He was feeding the cat.

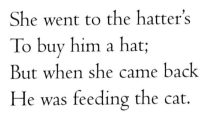

She went to the barber's
To buy him a wig;
But when she came back
He was dancing a jig.

She went to the tailor's
To buy him a coat;
But when she came back
He was riding a goat.

She went to the cobbler's
To buy him some shoes,
But when she came back
He was reading the news.

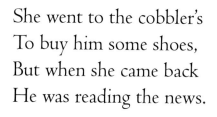

She went to the seamstress
To buy him some linen;
But when she came back
The dog was a-spinning.

She went to the hosier's
To buy him some hose;
But when she came back
He was dressed in his clothes.

The dame made a curtsy,
The dog made a bow;
The dame said, 'Your servant!'
The dog said, 'Bow-wow.'

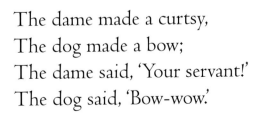

ONE, TWO, THREE, FOUR, FIVE

One, two, three, four, five,
    Once I caught a fish alive;
Six, seven, eight, nine, ten,
Then I let it go again.

Why did you let it go?
Because it bit my finger so.
Which finger did it bite?
This little finger on my right.

PUSSYCAT, PUSSYCAT

Pussycat, pussycat, where have you been?
   I've been up to London to look at the queen.
Pussycat, pussycat, what did you there?
I frightened a little mouse under her chair.

Repeat

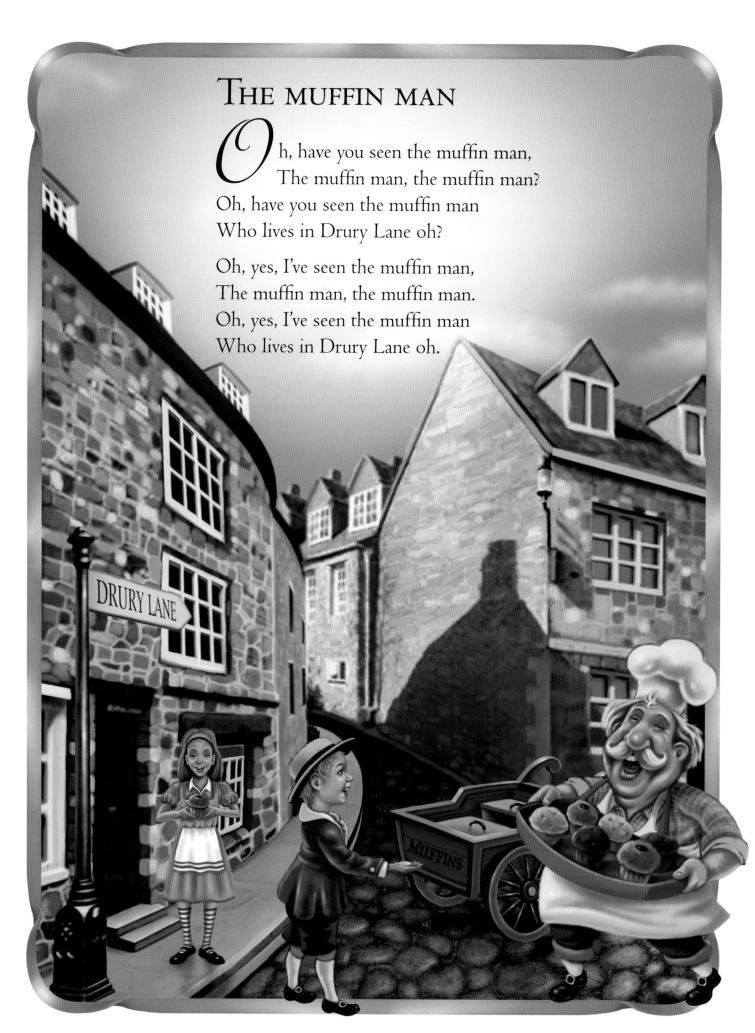

THE MUFFIN MAN

Oh, have you seen the muffin man,
The muffin man, the muffin man?
Oh, have you seen the muffin man
Who lives in Drury Lane oh?

Oh, yes, I've seen the muffin man,
The muffin man, the muffin man.
Oh, yes, I've seen the muffin man
Who lives in Drury Lane oh.

ROW, ROW, ROW YOUR BOAT

Row, row, row your boat,
Gently down the stream,
Merrily, merrily, merrily, merrily,
Life is but a dream.

Repeat

THERE WERE TEN IN THE BED

There were ten in the bed
And the little one said,
'Roll over! Roll over!'
So they all rolled over
And one fell out,
And he gave a little scream,
And he gave a little shout, 'Yahoo!'
Please remember to tie a knot in
    your pyjamas,
Single beds are only made for
One, two, three, four, five, six, seven, eight —

There were nine in the bed
And the little one said,
'Roll over! Roll over!'
So they all rolled over
And one fell out,
And he gave a little scream,
And he gave a little shout, 'Yahoo!'
Please remember to tie a knot in your pyjamas,
Single beds are only made for
One, two, three, four, five, six, seven —

There were eight in the bed
And the little one said,
'Roll over! Roll over!'
So they all rolled over
And one fell out,
And he gave a little scream,
And he gave a little shout, 'Yahoo!'
Please remember to tie a knot in your pyjamas,
Single beds are only made for
One, two, three, four, five, six —

There were seven in the bed
And the little one said,
'Roll over! Roll over!'
So they all rolled over
And one fell out,
And he gave a little scream,
And he gave a little shout, 'Yahoo!'
Please remember to tie a knot in
    your pyjamas,
Single beds are only made for
One, two, three, four, five —

There were six in the bed
And the little one said,
'Roll over! Roll over!'
So they all rolled over
And one fell out,
And he gave a little scream,
And he gave a little shout, 'Yahoo!'
Please remember to tie a knot in
    your pyjamas,
Single beds are only made for
One, two, three, four –

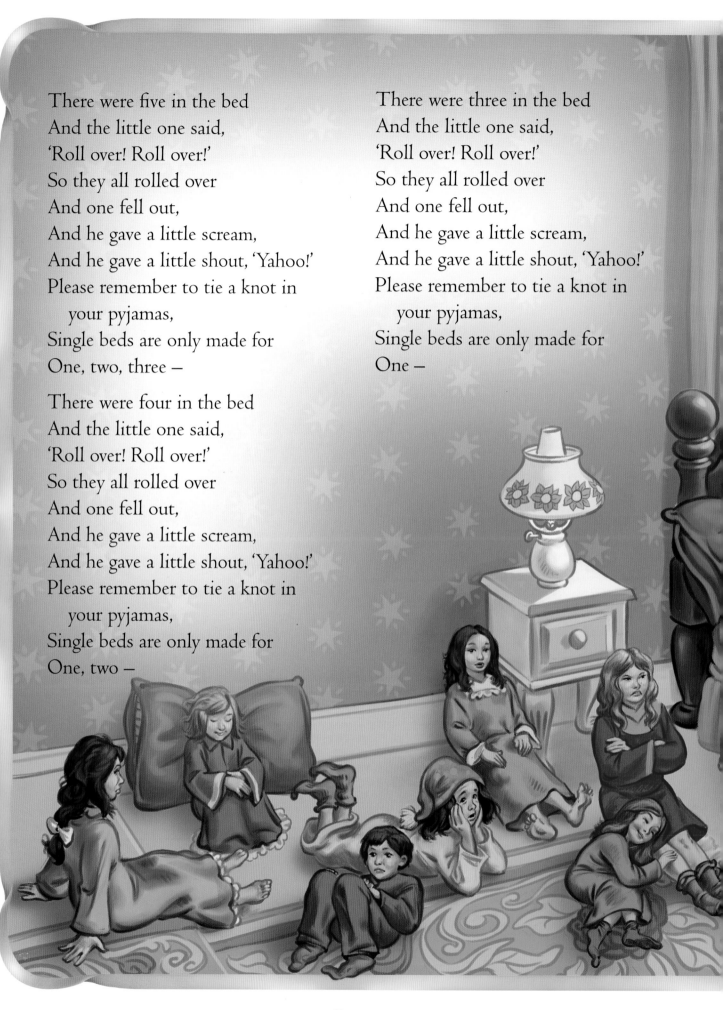

There were five in the bed
And the little one said,
'Roll over! Roll over!'
So they all rolled over
And one fell out,
And he gave a little scream,
And he gave a little shout, 'Yahoo!'
Please remember to tie a knot in
    your pyjamas,
Single beds are only made for
One, two, three —

There were four in the bed
And the little one said,
'Roll over! Roll over!'
So they all rolled over
And one fell out,
And he gave a little scream,
And he gave a little shout, 'Yahoo!'
Please remember to tie a knot in
    your pyjamas,
Single beds are only made for
One, two —

There were three in the bed
And the little one said,
'Roll over! Roll over!'
So they all rolled over
And one fell out,
And he gave a little scream,
And he gave a little shout, 'Yahoo!'
Please remember to tie a knot in
    your pyjamas,
Single beds are only made for
One —

There were two in the bed
And the little one said,
'Roll over! Roll over!'
So they all rolled over
And one fell out,
And he gave a little scream,
And he gave a little shout, 'Yahoo!'
Please remember to tie a knot in
    your pyjamas,
Single beds are only made for one.
Single beds are only made for one.

ORANGES AND LEMONS

'Oranges and lemons,'
   Say the bells of St Clements.

'You owe me five farthings,'
Say the bells of St Martins.

'When will you pay me?'
Say the bells of Old Bailey.

'When I grow rich,'
Say the bells at Shoreditch.

'When will that be?'
Say the bells of Stepney.

'I'm sure I don't know,'
Says the great bell at Bow.

Here comes the candle to light you to bed,
Here comes the chopper to chop off your head,
Chip chop, chip chop, the last man's head!

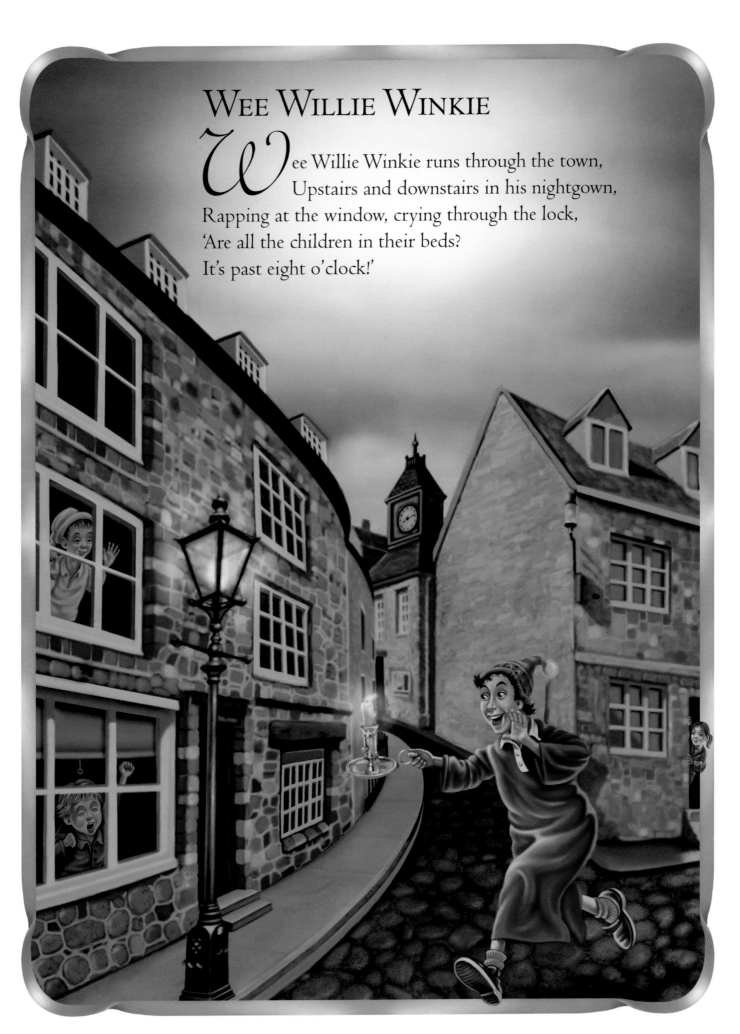

WEE WILLIE WINKIE

Wee Willie Winkie runs through the town,
    Upstairs and downstairs in his nightgown,
Rapping at the window, crying through the lock,
'Are all the children in their beds?
It's past eight o'clock!'

LITTLE BO-PEEP

Little Bo-Peep has lost her sheep,
And doesn't know where to find them;
Leave them alone, and they'll come home,
Dragging their tails behind them.

Little Bo-Peep fell fast asleep,
And dreamed she heard them bleating;
But when she woke 'twas all a joke,
For they were still a-fleeting.

Then up she took her little crook,
And vowed that she would find them;
What was her joy to see them then,
Wagging their tails behind them.

POLLY PUT THE KETTLE ON

*P*olly, put the kettle on,
    Polly, put the kettle on,
Polly, put the kettle on,
We'll all have tea.

Sukey, take it off again,
Sukey, take it off again,
Sukey, take it off again,
They've all gone away.

LITTLE JACK HORNER

*L*ittle Jack Horner
Sat in a corner,
Eating his Christmas pie;
He put in his thumb,
And pulled out a plum,
And said, 'What a
good boy am I!'

THE ANIMALS WENT IN TWO BY TWO

The animals went in two by two,
Hurrah! Hurrah!
The animals went in two by two,
Hurrah! Hurrah!
The animals went in two by two,
The elephant and the kangaroo.
And they all went into the ark
For to get out of the rain.

The animals went in three by three,
Hurrah! Hurrah!
The animals went in three by three,
Hurrah! Hurrah!
The animals went in three by three,
The wasp, the ant and the bumblebee.
And they all went into the ark
For to get out of the rain.

The animals went in four by four,
Hurrah! Hurrah!
The animals went in four by four,
Hurrah! Hurrah!

The animals went in four by four,
The great hippopotamus stuck in the door.
And they all went into the ark
For to get out of the rain.

The animals went in five by five,
Hurrah! Hurrah!
The animals went in five by five,
Hurrah! Hurrah!
The animals went in five by five,
They felt so happy to be alive.
And they all went into the ark
For to get out of the rain.

The animals went in six by six,
Hurrah! Hurrah!
The animals went in six by six,
Hurrah! Hurrah!
The animals went in six by six,
They turned out the monkey
    because of his tricks.
And they all went into the ark
For to get out of the rain.

The animals went in seven by seven,
Hurrah! Hurrah!
The animals went in seven by seven,
Hurrah! Hurrah!
The animals went in seven by seven,
The little pig thought he was going
    to heaven.
And they all went into the ark
For to get out of the rain.

The animals went in eight by eight,
Hurrah! Hurrah!
The animals went in eight by eight,
Hurrah! Hurrah!
The animals went in eight by eight,
The slithery snake slid under the gate.
And they all went into the ark
For to get out of the rain.

The animals went in nine by nine,
Hurrah! Hurrah!
The animals went in nine by nine,
Hurrah! Hurrah!

The animals went in nine by nine,
The rhino stood on the porcupine.
And they all went into the ark
For to get out of the rain.

The animals went in ten by ten,
Hurrah! Hurrah!
The animals went in ten by ten,
Hurrah! Hurrah!
The animals went in ten by ten,
And Noah said, 'Let's start again!'
And they all went into the ark
For to get out of the rain.

SIMPLE SIMON

Simple Simon met a pieman,
 Going to the fair;
Says Simple Simon to the pieman,
'Let me taste your ware.'

Says the pieman to Simple Simon,
'Show me first your penny';
Says Simple Simon to the pieman,
'Indeed, I have not any.'

Simple Simon went a-fishing,
For to catch a whale;
All the water he had got
Was in his mother's pail.

Simple Simon went to look
If plums grew on a thistle;
He pricked his fingers very much,
Which made poor Simon whistle.

PETER, PETER, PUMPKIN EATER

Peter, Peter, pumpkin eater,
      Had a wife and couldn't keep her;
He put her in a pumpkin shell,
And there he kept her very well.

Peter, Peter, pumpkin eater,
Had another and didn't love her;
Peter learned to read and spell,
And then he loved her very well.

SING A SONG OF SIXPENCE

Sing a song of sixpence,
A pocket full of rye;
Four and twenty blackbirds
Baked in a pie.

When the pie was opened
The birds began to sing;
Wasn't that a dainty dish
To set before the king?

The king was in his counting-house
Counting out his money;
The queen was in the parlour
Eating bread and honey.

The maid was in the garden
Hanging out the clothes,
When down came a blackbird,
And pecked off her nose.

But then came a jenny wren
And popped it on again.

LITTLE BOY BLUE

Little Boy Blue,
Come blow your horn,
The sheep's in the meadow,
The cow's in the corn.

But where is the boy
Who looks after the sheep?
He's under a haystack,
Fast asleep.

Will you wake him?
No, not I,
For if I do,
He's sure to cry.

DIDDLE, DIDDLE, DUMPLING, MY SON JOHN

Diddle, diddle, dumpling, my son John,
Went to bed with his trousers on;
One shoe off, and the other shoe on,
Diddle, diddle, dumpling, my son John.

I SAW THREE SHIPS

I saw three ships come sailing by,
    Come sailing by, come sailing by,
I saw three ships come sailing by,
On Christmas Day in the morning.

And what do you think was in them then,
Was in them then, was in them then?
And what do you think was in them then,
On Christmas Day in the morning?

Three pretty girls were in them then,
Were in them then, were in them then,
Three pretty girls were in them then,
On Christmas Day in the morning.

One could whistle, and one could sing,
And one could play on the violin;
So joy there was at my wedding,
On Christmas Day in the morning.

THERE WAS A CROOKED MAN

There was a crooked man, and he walked a crooked mile,
    He found a crooked sixpence against a crooked stile:
He bought a crooked cat, which caught a crooked mouse,
And they all lived together in a little crooked house.

THE GRAND OLD DUKE OF YORK

Oh, the grand old Duke of York,
He had ten thousand men;
He marched them up to the top of the hill,
And he marched them down again.

Chorus:

And when they were up, they were up,
And when they were down, they were down;
And when they were only halfway up,
They were neither up nor down.

Oh, the grand old Duke of York,
He had ten thousand men;
They beat their drums to the top of the hill,
And they beat them down again.

Chorus

One, Two, Buckle My Shoe

One, two, buckle my shoe;

Three, four, knock on the door;

Five, six, pick up sticks;

Seven, eight, lay them straight;

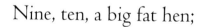

Nine, ten, a big fat hen;

Eleven, twelve, dig and delve;

Thirteen, fourteen, maids a-courting;

Fifteen, sixteen, maids in the kitchen;

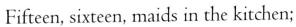

Seventeen, eighteen, maids in waiting;

Nineteen, twenty, my plate's empty.

Repeat

I HAD A LITTLE NUT TREE

I had a little nut tree,
　　Nothing would it bear
But a silver nutmeg
And a golden pear.

The King of Spain's daughter
Came to visit me,
And all for the sake
Of my little nut tree.

I skipped over water,
I danced over sea;
And all the birds in the air
Couldn't catch me!

A TISKET, A TASKET

A tisket, a tasket,
A green and yellow basket.
I wrote a letter to my love,
But on the way I dropped it.
I dropped it, I dropped it,
And on the way, I dropped it.
A little boy picked it up,
And put it in his pocket.

THREE BLIND JELLYFISH

Three blind jellyfish, three blind jellyfish,
Three blind jellyfish, sitting on a rock.
Then one fell off! ... Uh-oh!

Two blind jellyfish, two blind jellyfish,
Two blind jellyfish, sitting on a rock.
Then one fell off! ... Uh-oh!

One blind jellyfish, one blind jellyfish,
One blind jellyfish, sitting on a rock.
Then one fell off! ... Uh-oh!

No blind jellyfish, no blind jellyfish,
No blind jellyfish, sitting on a rock.
Then one jumped on! ... Hooray!

One blind jellyfish, one blind jellyfish,
One blind jellyfish, sitting on a rock.
Here comes another one! ... Hooray!

Two blind jellyfish, two blind jellyfish,
Two blind jellyfish, sitting on a rock.
Here comes another one! ... Hooray!

Three blind jellyfish, three blind jellyfish,
Three blind jellyfish, sitting on a rock.
Hooray!

THREE LITTLE KITTENS

Three little kittens, they lost their mittens,
And they began to cry;
Oh, mother dear, we sadly fear
That we have lost our mittens.
What! Lost your mittens, you naughty kittens!
Then you shall have no pie.
Mee-ow, mee-ow, mee-ow,
No, you shall have no pie.

Three little kittens, they found their mittens,
And they began to cry;
Oh, mother dear, see here, see here,
For we have found our mittens.
Put on your mittens, you silly kittens,
And you shall have some pie.
Purr-r, purr-r, purr-r,
Oh, let us have some pie.

Three little kittens put on their mittens,
And soon ate up the pie;
Oh, mother dear, we greatly fear
That we have soiled our mittens.
What! Soiled your mittens, you naughty kittens!
Then they began to sigh,
Mee-ow, mee-ow, mee-ow,
Then they began to sigh.

The three little kittens, they washed their mittens,
And hung them out to dry;
Oh, mother dear, do you not hear
That we have washed our mittens?
What! Washed your mittens, you good little kittens,
But I smell a rat close by.
Mee-ow, mee-ow, mee-ow,
We smell a rat close by.

SALLY, GO ROUND THE SUN

Sally, go round the sun,
    Sally, go round the moon,
Sally, go round the chimneypots,
On a Saturday afternoon.

Repeat

TO MARKET, TO MARKET

To market, to market, to buy a fat pig,
Home again, home again, jiggety-jig;
To market, to market, to buy a fat hog,
Home again, home again, jiggety-jog.

MONKEYS ON THE BED

Three little monkeys
    Jumping on the bed;
One fell off
And bumped his head.
Mummy rang the doctor and
The doctor said:
'No more monkeys
Jumping on the bed.'

Do your ears hang low?

Do your ears hang low?
　　Do they wobble to and fro?
Can you tie them in a knot?
Can you tie them in a bow?
Can you throw them over your shoulder,
Like a regimental soldier?
Do your ears hang low?

Number one, tickle your tum

umber one, tickle your tum,

Number two, just say 'Boo!'

Number three, touch your knee,

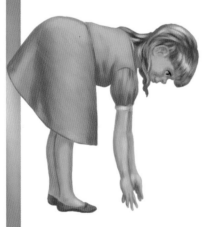

Number four, touch the floor,

Number five, do a dive,

Number six, wriggle your hips,

Number seven, jump to heaven,

Number eight, stand up straight,

Number nine, walk in a line,

Number ten, do it all again!

Repeat

THE BIG SHIP SAILS ON THE ALLEY, ALLEY O

The big ship sails on the alley, alley O,
The alley, alley O, the alley, alley O.
The big ship sails on the alley, alley O,
On the last day of September.

The captain said, 'It will never, never do,
Never never do, never never do.'
The captain said, 'It will never, never do,'
On the last day of September.

The big ship sank to the bottom of the sea,
The bottom of the sea, the bottom of the sea,
The big ship sank to the bottom of the sea,
On the last day of September.

We all dip our heads in the deep, blue sea.
The deep, blue sea, the deep, blue sea.
We all dip our heads in the deep, blue sea,
On the last day of September.

I LOVE LITTLE PUSSY

I love little pussy, her coat is so warm,
　　And if I don't hurt her she'll do me no harm.
So I'll not pull her tail, nor drive her away,
But pussy and I very gently will play.

STAR WISH

Star light, star bright,
First star I see tonight,
I wish I may, I wish I might,
Have the wish I wish tonight.

Repeat

ROCK-A-BYE, BABY, ON THE TREE TOP

Rock-a-bye, baby, on the tree top,
When the wind blows, the cradle will rock;
When the bough breaks, the cradle will fall,
And down will come baby, cradle and all.

TWINKLE, TWINKLE, LITTLE STAR

Twinkle, twinkle, little star,
How I wonder what you are!
Up above the world so high,
Like a diamond in the sky.

Chorus:

Twinkle, twinkle, little star,
How I wonder what you are!

When the blazing sun is gone,
When he nothing shines upon,
Then you show your little light,
Twinkle, twinkle, all the night.

Chorus

Then the traveller in the dark,
Thanks you for your tiny spark,
Could he see which way to go,
If you did not twinkle so?

Chorus

In the dark blue sky you keep,
While you through my curtains peep,
And you never shut your eye,
Till the sun is in the sky.

Chorus

Hush, little baby

Hush, little baby, don't say a word,
Papa's going to buy you a mockingbird.

If that mockingbird won't sing,
Papa's going to buy you a diamond ring.

If that diamond ring turns brass,
Papa's going to buy you a looking glass.

If that looking glass gets broke,
Papa's going to buy you a billy goat.

If that billy goat won't pull,
Papa's going to buy you a cart and bull.

If that cart and bull turn over,
Papa's going to buy you a dog named Rover.

If that dog named Rover won't bark,
Papa's going to buy you a horse and cart.

If that horse and cart fall down,
You'll still be the sweetest little baby in town.

SLEEP, BABY, SLEEP

Sleep, baby, sleep,
    Thy father tends the sheep,
Thy mother rocks the slumber tree,
And softly falls a dream for thee.
Sleep, baby, sleep.

BRAHMS' LULLABY

Lullaby and goodnight,
With roses bestride,
With lilies bedecked,
'Neath baby's sweet bed.

May thou sleep, may thou rest,
May thy slumber be blest.
May thou sleep, may thou rest,
May thy slumber be blest.

Lullaby and goodnight,
Thy mother's delight.
Bright angels around,
My darling, shall guard.

They will guide thee from harm,
Thou art safe in my arms.
They will guide thee from harm,
Thou art safe in my arms.

Johannes Brahms

The End